DKMH

DKMH

Dacre Montgomery

Andrews McMeel
PUBLISHING®

DKMH

"This, the minutia; my life.

I am a STALLION; bipolar.

I just reached contact with a lost nation; another person.
A different relation.

A different time and a different patience.

As if I've cried in a dream, woken up screaming; then settled
in the sheets.

I find both connection and softness. A lost tension, now
tempered with aged awareness."

Dacre Montgomery

I want to thank my Mother and my Love
for giving me the courage.

My entire life I have felt fragile. Overexposed, especially as a child.

I felt I had a softness. Like I had no shield from the emotional intensity of the world. Both in a good way and a bad way.
I felt profoundly affected by even the smallest of things.
I suffered from terrible anxiety.
I knew not how to harness this energy. The energy I would later discover was the most powerful and valuable thing in the entire world.

When I was younger, I didn't have the outlets that I have today. I lacked work ethic. I didn't play sports or exercise. I had no independence to discover what these feelings meant.

Granted, that discovery has manifested itself in different ways over the years . . . I was a late bloomer.

At seventeen I discovered alcohol and partying—an outlet I thought would be useful. But time and time again, I found myself anxious the next day, even after one drink. The alcohol dimmed my light.

While others chased the feeling of ecstasy through outlets like drugs, drink, and sex, I have always felt like I could achieve that feeling without the aid of substance. In school I could talk about music and architecture, film and design, and goose bumps would ripple across my skin. I felt like I could self-induce that feeling of ecstasy.

Though epiphanies would not come daily until I was older,
I felt as though I had a bottomless pit of passion.
I would lock myself in my room and watch film after film.
I lived my childhood (largely) through the escapism of
cinema, and what I didn't know then but came to know as . . .
manifestation.

My imagination ran wild and I started to harness . . .

Like a sorcerer I started to use the energy gifted to me.
The energy that had me in fits as a child. The energy
that had given me sleepless nights or dysfunctional
relationships with those around me. Those who had
called my bluffs, bullied me, or put me down—I started to
use their energy. The negative energy and the light in my
life both fueled me.

My OCD manifested itself in my room, meticulously
cleaning house. Although my OCD was dysfunctional,
I started to set goals and work out. I started to harness
this energy.

I manifested and I imagined other worlds more and more.

When I first fell in love, I fell hard. Like an asteroid the
size of Africa, breaking the atmosphere and pummeling
a million miles an hour toward the surface of the earth.
I obsessed . . . because I am obsessive over everything.

The first love brought fire and I raged. I loved. I burned.

Melancholy hits me hard. Sentimentality strikes deep. It hurts me. I feel so affected by everyone and everything. I train hard, to shut it out sometimes, and other times I feel vulnerable and I use it. In my acting and in my life.

I love to dive deep sometimes and depression has hit hard more than once and stayed longer than I would have liked.

Like I said, when I'm happy, it's ecstasy, and when I'm sad, it's a dark force that I have let reaper me.

I had never written a thing before. So poetry had a roundabout way of injecting itself into my life.

I had been reading scripts for two years and had become increasingly interested in story structure and words. The beautiful power of description.

Some of my favorite writers are gifted with emotional engagement and they are word wizards. Master craftspeople of the art of dicing up the meat of the English language and expertly serving it on platters of tears and joy to the masses.

Each day for about two months, I went to the same coffee shop and I studied our language.

Little did I know at the time, this was to become another coping mechanism. As a cook finds solace and meditation in cooking, I was finding my ingredients for a fruitful alleviant of the pressures and wonders of my world.

. . . I never wrote a thing though.
I guess in hindsight my body was waiting. Waiting for my world to shift and ground to shake. For that meteor to crest the horizon and to make meat of my heart. I was waiting to bathe in electricity and to be shattered like glass. "To wonder, to ask, to fall."
Not long after, I was—deeply.

After a first date, which seemed fate, I came home. One night passed, then another.
Then something happened—at my parents' home, late in the afternoon . . . I began something. A journey that has not stopped since. The bottle rocket shot deep into me. And I've never looked back.

I began to write. Assisted by the sound of Desert Wind . . . quite literally. A smartphone app that provided nature sounds became my Sherpa through the unknown valleys of my emotions. We set off . . .

That night, the words poured out of me. I felt as though I was shedding layers.

I mentioned in my opening quote "bipolar". . . I felt as though I was someone else and at the same time more myself than ever before.

The imagery I write comes in colors in my head; . . . hallucinations.

Then it comes in a feeling; hot and cold flashes.

The first page is gobbledygook. Just rantings, trying to tap into a well of emotions.

Some days I would write about love or loss. Whether something had happened in my life or I woke in the middle of the night called by some unknown entity. I knew not.

But I certainly can't just write. I have to be affected, otherwise the well is dry.
I have to feel fragile enough to be connected to these words.

These poems are moments in my life; defining notes I have conducted in my internal orchestra. I am so pleased to be sharing them with you.
They are personal, but I'm sure universal of what makes me/you/everyone human.

PLAYLIST

Sound has been my guiding force, whether be nature
or music.
So a playlist seems only fitting . . . Should you so choose
to use it.

Music tethers me to these words and conjures all my senses.

In a time when music is so freely accessible I thought it a
pertinent accompaniment to this book.

I will suggest the following albums to accompany the read.
I will tell you what I see and feel . . .

NICK DRAKE—Bryter Layter
This, the morning.
Trees cast dabbled sunlight on the dining table.
No one is up except the birds. The wind is still asleep.
I have started my day with this album for the last
ten years.
It knows me, but I'm still curious about it. Notes I've
not yet noticed.
<u>This music knows me.</u>

JOHN MARTYN—Solid Air
This, midday.
Electric. Eccentric. The day is at a roar. Traffic whips past.
I am fueled. The sky is blue. Picture perfect. I write.
I ponder. I circle the balcony and breathe the crisp air.
My garden is green. The colors are rich, ignited by
the warmth.
<u>This music feeds me.</u>

GETZ/GILBERTO—Stan Getz & João Gilberto
This, the evening.
Lit by candlelight. I smell cedar. The sun setting, casts
brilliant pink hues through the kitchen.
I feel warm and cool at the same time. Hair wet from
a shower.
Clean linen is soft on my skin.
I hear laughter. Food brings us together and conversation
keeps us there.
<u>This music softens me.</u>

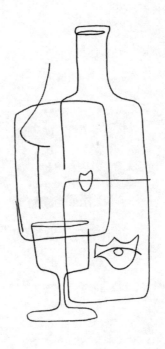

FEAR

A vivid dream that came as a whole puzzle.
You just lost a piece.

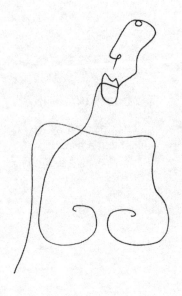

Mask stripped
Kerosene lipped
Striking against flint.

Legs, pistons. Coal powered.
Steam engine, freight train.
That clicker, clacker of refrain.
Pistol-whip.
Jugular-hit.

The lens flipped.
To admit, a visage
Of fishbowl shape
Distorted vape.
The smoke cloud moved and changed its
shape.

It's always in bed. In sleep.

In night. Wake with a fright.

Washed over like splashes of boiling
water singeing my skin.

Where have I been?   To a place far
away, in some clandestine bay.

Vision of grandeur turned delusions of
something that I was supposed to obey.

Mercury bisque.
White like halogen
Opaque like a curtain
Speckled like a freckle
Tested like a medal

That political stigma
The plaintiff is here
The jury is out
Heart filled with fear.

For it is your life
That is the enigma.

For they will find you're a liar
And figure out your every fear
Put on a brave face
But you're just a deer

Caught in headlights
9/10 lashes away from a discovery won't set
you apart
                              You're a part of an
uncovering
That leads to an unraveling

I did a lot of work to get here.
Suppressing of a type
Only the pressure of the ocean could
match
Even then, a mile down
NO equalizing could thatch
Away at that cauldron
                    That's been
bubbling bubbling.

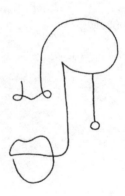

I did a lot of work to get here.
    Battle ropes
    Kriss-Kross
In and out of frame.
Right, left.
Robbery—theft.
You robbed me of a childhood.
Innocent and free.
You robbed and bribed me of my naivety.

Hand to Hand.
           Passed down.
A generational misstep rooted.
Roots thick, rotten, and twisted.

An inheritance of irony and pain.

Gene pool rippled.
Did you fall in?
Or did you plummet to your destiny
An ascent of alchemy
A concoction of your own making
A path changing, ever changing.

Pasted, jaded. Time has flown by, my
memories faded. It's hard to walk, it's
hard to breathe, it's hard to talk.

The fallacy you made myth, I turned
legend. It was all a lie from the
beginning. I ain't no legend.

You weren't born; C-section cut from the
stomach of an IVF. Virgin turned myth,
turned legend.

The world knows, the world sees, the
world heralds a king and destroys the
child.

Take it away from me   he he he -
don't laugh at he.

He's human and trying   Trying to long
and hold and close in
In and in.

Inside of you

pouring in.

Street light light, covered from fog in the
night night.

It's like an egg atop a crown. It fell down
and cracked and bent out of shape and
began to create
something small crawling and yawning
and forming.

I growl at it, faint-hearted fool. I growl
at you, let me out of this pool.

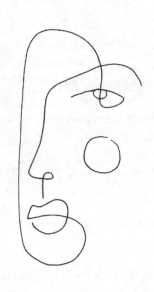

Spaghetti

Circle circle, round, circle

Egos and she goes

Walk right up and round

Round pendulum swinging and it's beginning to look a lot like Christmas

White, strike one two and me   You're out.

Ego, wherever she goes you go she goes

Going past the clouds, through the rip

In the sky so high.

Brown and Orange Orange is loose and warm and ripples

Like juice.

Cools you, aids you.

That sodium vapor.
Your heart seems safer.
Mine is thin, like paper
Rolls like a thistle
Sharpened like a fossil
Whittled like a stick
Rhubarb crumble
Sweet and thick.

Whisper in my ear. Whisper me secrets.
Make me warm and my senses tingle
That first night, why I saw your skin
gleaming and your eyes were beaming

Whisper me ok's and loves and
happiness

Whisper me the plural of love

Durable love,

spacious, contagious

As if I'm locked in a basement filled with
water. That last bit of air is eating me
from the inside out.

I close my eyes.
        I open my eyes.

Just to make sure.
  That I made it here.
I pocket the sand.
Brush off my hand.
Just to make sure.
  That I made it here.

I eat the nectar, of the sweet.
I bathe in the ombre sky.
I block my ears under the shower.

Just to feel. In this hour. The power. Of
making it here.
Going clear.

LOVE

Now this, I give to you. My flower.

To ask, to wonder, to fall.

Some moments.

Some moments are like pain.
Some moments are like happy.
Some stick in your brain.
Some moments take decades.
Some moments go past in the blink of an
eye.
Some moments never stop.
Like this one with you and I.

In a moment you made me collapse.
You made my heart shake and memory
lapse.
I forgot of a time before and ahead.
My limbs seemed to collapse.
In a moment you made me forget the
pain.
My fear stoked and disappeared.

In a moment I was equalized by you.
You.
My heroine, had saved the day.

And now, every moment seems new.
And you, the glue.

Though destiny had shown me her face I
was stopped, stammered in this place.

I turned to you, put my hand on yours.

Smooth like silk, warm like bed. I
softened and moved toward your head.

I proclaimed my desire, like a
Shakespearian fable

And then after merely a moment, put
everything on the table.

We kissed. It was simple, it was bliss.

You had me.

My heart was in your hand, before you
could even understand.

Like a sorcerer I wish I could bend time

Make malleable my fate and open up my mind.

I wish I could summon color.

If I could

I'd seduce turquoise and dark blues

If I could

I'd wrap up purple and similar hues

If I could summon color I'd give it all to you.

I'd make air sweet.

I'd make our space neat.

I'd make our bed a cupcake.

I'd make our life complete.

I'd join the scouts.
Just to learn about knots.
So I could undo
Every ball I ever made.
I'd be able to undo the ones
In your stomach
The ones that give you pain
And those ones wrapped up in your
brain.

You're a map Navel right up your back.
Toes, to the top of the stack.

Tires stop, engine hot, hands on the
wheel time stood still, then rushed
forward.

Western sun, split shadows across your
lawn. White door opened and I saw a
perfect form.

T'was you, I kept poised, profile forward.
Scared, can she see me?

My if's and but's, came to a halt. Your
hand cradled the door, then a jolt, open.

I saw your bronze skin, the door opening
and in

Leg first

White skirt   softening.

Without a word, without flirting, you
sunk in

Seats like buckets, flowing over the brim.

Then t'was you, poised, profile forward.
Scared? No, you turn and look me
through.

I had never seen someone like you.
Pierced me, daggers of blue.

Topaz forests. With a trillion cut edges.
The pressures of life, had forced out a
diamond.

Earth's rarest, sat a mere foot from my
ear. Then she spoke, without a choke or
moment of fear.

We travel through the day Making our
way up the brown lines of the earth

Exploring many areas.

Some new.

Some old.

We eat   bold.

Eyes locked in an unfamiliar mold.

Can't peel away, like an orange, citrus
cracking under the pressure No, you're
more like a sweet peach, nothing to
measure. Except sweet, when our eyes
meet.

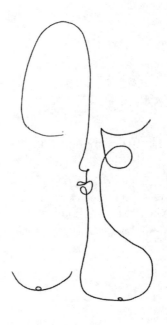

No sleep came as they danced dancing
in the form he took for a moment or two,
for a day or two in June.

The heat came in waves, staved off the
sweat, broke an intense bet

            not to love, not to fall in
love.

Mud, sweat, tears, teeth, goose bumps
rippled across my skin, felt like nothing
else mattered and didn't need to know
where to begin.

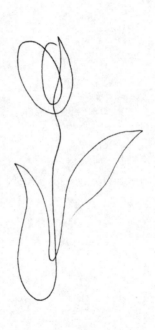

Trying not to idolize too much, swimming
in your pool, not putting you on a
pedestal. Pedi, ready, steady, go . . .

To be recognized for one's true self, past
the facade and all that marmalade sugar-
covered business that can be a
distracting business. Past the cars,
seeing up and over and through all of the
stars. I've sipped from your cup, but
now I'm stuck.

And I don't know when to give up.

Can smell your soul aching,
Cologne fading,
My stomach flips
Butterflies, eclipse

We eat, we fuck, we sleep, sleeping for
the first time in a week.

Merged energy, energy is a
collaboration, three rings bound, without
a sound.

Maleficent beauty, blonde cheeks, cheeks
and then begins to speak, splitting sound.

Voice like butter, baking a cake, three
parts desire, one part fire.

DKMH

I was selfish to a point, two years past
03, then I met you and it was you and me.

Bound hip, heart and hand, hand in
hand, hand in the sand on a beach.

Tobacco is the smell of fire, on your
clothes, in your pores, it stores and stays.

Ringing in your ears, outside a club,
can't hear you, but I see you, clearly.

I begin to paint.

You through three different lenses.

Stroke a course to the east, across the
Nullarbor.

Fingers calloused and heart sore.

I brush west, feel the cool breeze.

The ocean salt and my backyard trees.

I feel the hasty call   a rush to tea.

I change color, as I paint.

The art, the paint. The fuck of it all.

A-mart, the saint. The muck of it all.

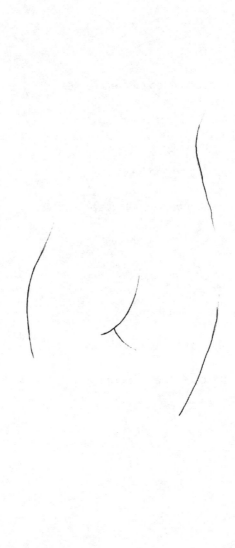

Opaque, cloudy, can't quite make out
    what I seem to think you're about.

Weaved, woven, knitted together like a
sweater
    for the coldest weather.
Tight, but soft and warm.

Idle I wait.
    For that heartbeat. For she, to see,
to see he, who wants to explore.
To explore more, more of her heartbeat,
her heartbeat that is the world.

Distance, in body but not mind. How
sublime it must be to think like he.
    He, is not me, though how I wish to
be as simple, and as free.

      Burdens are a gift. Thrifted from
the greatest of he's and she's and
bestowed upon me.

      To see, to feel. Burdened by
insecurity. The irony.   Ashamed
to have blamed that peach nose and
sphere world heart.

I know parts of you, but like the world
with its vastness. Its beauty. I have not
tasted all of you. You trapped and draped
your silk skin, around me. Not him.
Silently I listen in.

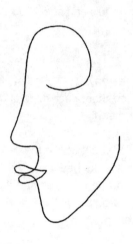

A complex puzzle. Centuries have tried to
figure you out.
But there is no figuring you out.
You are without a doubt,
the biggest mystery of all.   You are
complex and simple
and unpredictable.   You are the waves,
the tides, and current.
Born of the sea, a complete mystery.

The dreams I had about you, were
    For a moment real, we got to live
The unbroken seal.
No restraint.

Short and sweet.
Honey and wheat.

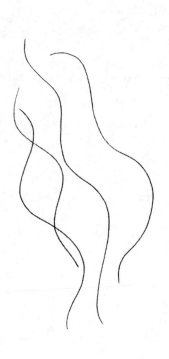

My moon.
    My moon.
       My moon.
     Why did I have to leave so soon.

ANXIETY

Shattered me like glass.

TV dinners and wicked sinners.

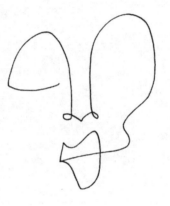

Control is the whirlwind
Wrapped in a puzzle
Words are the pieces
And your mouth the muzzle

DKMH

Pigment dyed and freeze fried
A vat of ray-on and cray-ons

Your OCD painted you a rainbow
Of coded, sized and alphabetized.

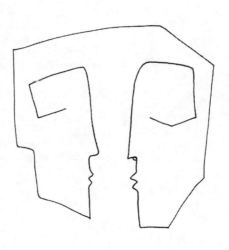

He wakes in the middle of the night, his
heart begins to fight, with his mind.

Fallacy became reality, reality became
sanity, sanity strained.

Strained, strained, strained.

To maintain his head, head was an atlas,
atlas broke his spine, then his mind.

Dopamine, produced too much, couldn't
let go.

The high was too high,

to say goodbye to the things we had
before they went.

My body is so spent,

dripping sweat, kitchen sink, blood on my
teeth.

Aching mind, splitting skulls, sleepless
nights.

Trying to quell,

quell what I got.

God-given energy, rife force, bumping
through my bloodstream, red blood cells.

Clot, stop, it's all tangled in one place,
nowhere to go, the pace has slowed.

Heartbeat stops, a ticking clock, three
cuckoos past the cuckoo clock.

Under the skylight, in the fading light

Light weightlessness   sucked me up
Wishing I didn't feel so heavy and
covered in muck

Eyes heavy, the suitcases are full but my
pockets are empty,

Torn, sporadic, staccato motion my
veins pump, in and out like the ocean.

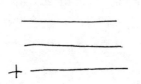

Pin dropped on the marble floor

The cold floor, the pin dropped

I cannot see it anymore

Disguised among the marble mass
chords stretched out onto the floor.

That flutter, stutter in my belly butter
goes only if for a moment I cannot ride
with this fear on my back feel the chords
go slack,

Six miles out and two from a heart attack

Static, static—stop-motion, feeling every
beat in this poisonous potion

Words uttered before resounding on the walls. Paper thin and yet no noise gets in.

The silence makes me quiver.

Spread apart. Anesthetized.

Numbed by separation. An incantation
of things to come.

Ratchet and rank. It's insane how much
is in the tank.

Colloquialisms of pain. At the forefront
of my brain.

My distaste, like rotten toothpaste in my
mouth, yelling out, behind my lungs

No air can get there, there is somewhere
far away from here from you to me

Bounce   bounce   bounce   the ball off
the wall.

Beating my head against a wall that's far
too tall

I'm screaming, underwater, drowning
and yelling. Aqua in my mouth my lungs
like jellyfish all water—no matter

why doesn't it matter

why doesn't it matter

why doesn't it matter

what I'm supposed to do. Why can't I
hear you

I'm screaming out.

Isolated and alone and blown—freezing.

Cracked like dry earth, when I speak
only—heaving

Some days I have a rose gold
breastplate.
Unencumbered by its weight.
Some days I have no armor at all.
And I just feel heavy and small.

Looming over the edge   Two fingers and
a thumb in a pledge

Burrowed deep, borrowed sleep.

Three things you have to do.
Live, love, die repeat

SPIRIT

The see-you-ess-pea.

"Don't think about it?"

    So, don't feel?
God, it must be so hard to not feel.
To deny yourself the will to feel.
To feel is to know things are real.
To feel is goose bumps, goose rippling
across your skin
Letting the reality in.
To feel is hot and cold and above all
vulnerable

Without feeling I am not a spirit.
Without spirit I am just   moving.

It is a thing, it is a funny thing to feel
your stomach, right into your spleen.

Cheers met, sounds of clinking glasses
as the sun sets.

Home, triangle roof, comfortable booth,
 feng shui oozes to the smell of
vermouth.

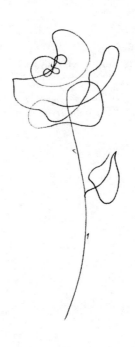

TLC, TLC, no man created me, me is not formed for society's sake, not a pinup.

Not a hunk, not junk and I have been sinking, sinking, but I'm afloat now, jumping off the boat.

Two rhymes, sixteen bars, a moment in time, to free, to speak, to seek, seek guidance.

Water and spiders, spiders spying a spider, spiders inside of her like a black hole.

That moment, hanging in opaque beauty.
The edge of a storm, something
withdrawn.

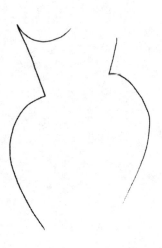

A jelly floats, moved with the tides.
Electric pulses keeping a body of water
in water alive.

I can hear it, The whistling, purring The
sound of the ocean Black stallion. She
roars, but a low hum. But I can hear it,
the sound of a drum.

Bah-dum, Bah-dum

Take me back, so I can hold it.

It is time, fine like sand. It dances and
falls through my hand.

Take me back,

      So I can feel it,

            Feel meeting a stranger.

We become the past and the present at the same time. In the twilight of our lives, we become the storytellers. The all-wise. The mature. Painted no color, but neutral. We are relaxed, we are softened. We made it. We are human.

Dacre Kayd Montgomery-Harvey is an Australian actor and poet, primarily known for his portrayal of Billy Hargrove in *Stranger Things*.

His podcast titled *DKMH* was released in 2019, rose to the top of podcast charts with over 1 million plays, and features his poetry paired with music from different musicians.

Born in Perth, Western Australia, Montgomery began performing in theater at the age of nine. He continued his studies in the dramatic arts in college, and received a degree in fine arts and acting in 2015. His poetry is an expression of what drives him, what scares him, what gets him up in the morning. Universal, instinctive, and deep, Montgomery's words touch hearts and minds across the globe.

Andrews McMeel Publishing
a division of Andrews McMeel Universal
1130 Walnut Street, Kansas City, Missouri 64106

www.andrewsmcmeel.com

20 21 22 23 24 RR2 10 9 8 7 6 5 4 3 2 1

ISBN: 978-1-5248-6165-0

Library of Congress Control Number: 2020941752

Illustrations by Sam Corlett

Editor: Patty Rice
Art Director/Designer: Julie Barnes
Production Editor: Dave Shaw
Production Manager: Cliff Koehler

ATTENTION: SCHOOLS AND BUSINESSES
Andrews McMeel books are available at quantity discounts with
bulk purchase for educational, business, or sales promotional use.
For information, please e-mail the Andrews McMeel Publishing
Special Sales Department: specialsales@amuniversal.com